It's Me. Again.

It's Me. Again.

L.N. Saleh

Matador
9 Priory Business Park,
Wistow Road, Kibworth Beauchamp,
Leicestershire. LE8 0RX
Tel: 0116 279 2299
Email: books@troubador.co.uk
Web: www.troubador.co.uk/matador
Twitter: @matadorbooks

ISBN 978 1800465 459

British Library Cataloguing in Publication Data.
A catalogue record for this book is available from the British Library.

Typeset in 10pt Minion Pro by Troubador Publishing Ltd, Leicester, UK

Matador is an imprint of Troubador Publishing Ltd

This book is dedicated to my brothers and sisters.
Life is better with you in it.

"If you can't be good, be quick." – Dave (1963-2020)

Contents

Acknowledgements

To my large and wonderful family. To my father, Fuad, my sisters Linda and Jodi and my brothers Peter and Jameel. To those we lost too soon: my mother, Helen, my brother, David, and our Aunt Meg. Thank you for always believing in me.

I wish to extend special thanks and gratitude to Suzanne Foster and her amazing children and grandchildren, Robert Macwhorter, Gareth Adeney, Lynn Kunstman and James Brodisky, Jenna Foster, Carole Lewthwaite, Douglas Allen, Jane and Jim Jeffries, Jean Storckman, Karm Hagedorn, Tom and Sheryl Lipski, Jason Couch, and Betty, Tommy and Jordan Thompson. Jolene Rydeen for the book cover design. Katie Farmer and Traci Buck for the author photo. Tara Hanby and Melanie Law for editing. Jennifer Dawn for the friendship.

I also wish to thank others for their support and hugs: the Flemings, Ashley and Caio, Nana, Bumper and Janet James Alman and Sheldon Alman, Jennifer Hankins, Carrie Dudley, Cindy Cameron, Maxine Graham, Laurel Banke, Laura Eggleston, Steve Rudall, and Eli Clarke. The staff at Southern Oregon Success Academy and Southbank International School.

Of course my nieces and nephews and their spouses who always keep me smiling: Jade, John, Bob, Erin, Chris, Lauren, Sam, Ben, Emily, Julia, Emmett, baby Erin... and just for the record, this bunch is so great that if more come our way, that would be wonderful.

Professionally, I need to acknowledge the following for their kindness, guidance, and influence: Bidita Sadiq, Nathalie Handel, Courtia Newland, Nimah Ismail Nawwab, Raman Mundair, Rommi Smith, Kadija George, and *Sable Literary Magazine* for the editing opportunity. Also Charlotte Hadella, Dave Moody, and Cindy Wallace from the Oregon Writing Project at Southern Oregon University, who got me off the starting block in regards to writing and publishing.

And to Mrs. Lorna Coleman, who was my high school English teacher, who encouraged me to write.

Lisa Nora Saleh
March 2021

Star Thrower

Remember me.

I am a star thrower.
If something bright and beautiful falls from the sky,
we find each other.

That is why I go from place to place.

Following a trail that leads to glowing cinders;
tenderly, I blow, revive.
Gentleness is the only force that can release the inner heat
from these embers, and
with proper care, these
dormant coals can heat for years.

Together,
we work,
till their hearts aglow.

Then one dark night
we'll both know
they need to return
to light another's path.

At that moment,
I throw the star back.

… It's
mE

Origins

In my blood I am a sheep herder.
Green hills on the Glens
become olive trees in a valley.
Bedouins on my paternal side.
Druids on the maternal.

Both races are people of the Earth.
Disciples of fate,
reading the future in the stars above.
Life depends on nature.
Love blooms in the wind,
warm soaked in
from footsteps on heated sand.

Welcoming breezes blow up from
the waterfalls and trout streams.

Originally,
neither side was devoted to a god.
Just to themselves,
their children
and their families.

Traditions following the seasons,
Life revolving with the sun.

Northern Ireland

Ina and Una are my sisters.
Paddy, our brother, is in London.
He sends money
to supplement the dole.
Too lazy to work, you say?
Untrue. Untrue.

We work every day,
walking the Glens,
lambing the ewes,
and eyeing the seas
that keep Ulster
away.

Seas that lock in lies and injustice.
Waves carrying tales that
there is no hope
for my land.
Belfast is beautiful.
Both the opera house
and city lights
beam bright.

Becoming home...
Her children
Forced out
By war
But not forgotten
Or ignored.

Ana

(I am)
Confessions of an Arab Woman

I revel in my secret happiness
every time I touch a cheek;
as soft as my own.
    Violin
its feminine shape
belongs in my arms
gentle strokes and caresses
compose sounds of pleasure.
A tune played together.
    Discreetly.
As a child, these joys
were mysteries.
My love concealed,
desires hushed,
fantasies altered,
each a part of my
cloaked existence.
    Generations
Gathered,
joined,
and produced
    Me.

In a garden of colour
an absence of unity
a dozen red roses
and a single white bud.
Whose beauty
    Needs
The
same sun
to blossom.

Wood Stove

Fire is security.
It warms my soul
as it heats my meals.

The farmhouse was our first wood stove.
Located under our bedroom,
we placed our feet on the grate for
warmth
and our ears to eavesdrop.

The next one we purchased as a family.
Travelling from the country to the city
my father simply pointed at it
and it appeared in our house.
In the mornings he awoke
and ignited the flame that
began our day.

Over a decade ago I moved
From my father's house and
I have been cold.

When I bought my own house,
it had no hearth,
and no heart.

Simple lesson learned,
nothing lives without one
and I don't belong in such a void.

My sanctuary came to me.
A simple stove,
flames enclosed in glass,
a mug of tea.
My heart,
my home.

A Bad Day Teaching

A bad day teaching is
a young man,
digging through a dumpster.
Who catches your eye as you walk by.
Suddenly, you remember that look from second-period English.

A tightly wound bodice
combined with spirited legs
that once performed for dance team medals,
and now only lift and twirl for cash.

Handcuffs clinking
during homeroom
locking in a six-year term
dispelling freedom.

Vomit; from a fourteen-year-old.
Hiding her morning sickness
in your classroom garbage can.

Holding her hair back, you hope
that your presence lessens her fears
because you have no answers to
her questions.

My worst day teaching
took place today.
At a graveside.
As a sixteen-year-old boy
was lowered into the ground.

A Simple Man

A low IQ
and a verbal
stutter
causes all to
stare
as he stammers

society jeers
and judges
him by his
Velcro Shoes
and fast-food
visor

every morning
he is grateful
for the warmth
of sun upon
his face

before getting
on the bus
he places coins and
a donut into
a homeless
man's hands

at work he greets
each customer with
a grin
in every task
he undertakes
he does his best.

Stuck

Boston to
Wisconsin;
museum to
farms.

Trading in
New England
clam chowder
for
Luthearn
beer batter
fish fry ups.

Peculiar accents
neither one
anywhere near
The same.

Knowing I
sound funny,
I try to look
good.

In the washroom
I tidy up
and realise
my zipper is
stuck.

In the down position
not up.

"Oh, my,
everyone will see,
how can they not!"

Looking for a place to hide
I sit in a stall to
decide, "Yes, leaving home is best."

"Perhaps, I have been forgotten?"

Footsteps in the corridor
alert me
to lift my feet.
My name echoes
off the graffiti on
the wall.

Above me I see,
my teacher's
hands and then
her nose and chin.

Her eyes ask mine,
"OK?"
and we both
know it
is not.

I motion to
my zipper,
my stomach
in a knot.

"Oh, dear, is that all?"
"I thought we had real trouble here."

Finally,
after stepping out,
a safety pin from
her bag
appears
to end my dilemma.

"Perhaps, I might
just stay after all."

Manure

The worst smell
you can imagine
is perfume to me.
Inhaling
growth and prosperity.

Childhood aroma
alfalfa and corn fields
Mom yelling through the screen door,
"Coop the chickens before dinner."

Tractor rides
stacking hay bales
dried feed corn and dust
pouring down the silo chute

My small fingers
poke gently through
afterbirth,
releasing a calf's
first breath.

Standing in awe
as they take their first
step

Pajamas with the
feet worn out
from running to the
barn.

Dressing up to bring
chickens for 4-H
to the state fair

returning with blue ribbons
stories of fried bread
and ferris wheels

Fall Festival
pie judging
fruit jam
and canned tomatoes
cow pie bingo in the town centre

The worst smell you can imagine
is perfume to me.

A small town with
one stoplight,
surrounded by fields and
guarded by volunteer firemen.

Two thousand people and
one succulent smell.

To the Women of the Central Point Twins Creek Outside Class

To the Women of the Central Point Twins Creek Outside Class:

Ladies, I salute you.
Marching away stress
dressed in leggings, socks and
a t-shirt stained with Gerber Apple Sauce.

Collaborated rhythm
punching away
the strain of the day.

Forgetting about
hassles, tangles, the
school pick up or was it the drop off?
Getting dinners done, over and over again
all while logged into the Zoom time delay.

Ladies, I salute you.
Swinging your arms in joy
while smiling in unity.
Overworked,
underpaid,
yet still kicking away.

Coming together
in jogging bras,
revealing stretch marks,
and yes, a few in Depends.

Ladies, I salute you.
Dancing,
twirling,
swaying
in female companionship.
A mutual support group
just to get each other
through another day.

Lessons from My Singing Teacher

Breathe.
Hum.
Laugh some.

Drink water.
Stand taller.
Smile.
Dance.
Repeat.

Practice.
Have fun.
Feel joy.
Find peace.

... It's
mE.
...Again.

Anti-Love

I forgo love.
I've had it.
I'm through.
Men and women alike,
you're both
one and the
same —
nothing but trouble,
trouble
and
pain!
I've been used,
lied to,
and yes,
even abused.
I've been cheated on,
not once,
but twice
and let me tell you,
Neither time was nice.
Oh, my God, what a bust
and it never ends just.
I'm telling you,
I'm tired,
I'm drained,
And I'm outta the game!
555-3782

Lennon's Paradise

*A poem dedicated to Dusty, a man who'd rather be met at the Pearly
Gates by John Lennon than Saint Peter. And I hope he was.*

Some things are
bigger than me.
Not many but a few,
if you have the time, right now.

I'll tell you about
one
or two.

Now, I know what you're thinking
and I've had that thought, too,
she'll just stand and say
a house, yes, of course,

so obvious to me
and to you.

No, that's not right.
It's not about size.

But a moral,
and one we can never
disguise.

Such as,
when being fair
and just,
isn't going to be considered
being square.

Imagine if you can,
a society
where might does not
make right
and there's no need
to fight.

A place not far from here.
Where everyone's got
a clean place to sleep,
three hots,
and all their shots.

Because that's
all we really need
to be fair,
and to be decent;
everywhere.

Shall I stand
and compare
you to
me?

Does it do me any good,
or you?
No, it does not.

It's terrible to think that
once we fought
about
food,
water,
oil,
all we wanted to do was
divide up the spoils.

So much easier
to just share,
then we'd all have some
here on our plates.
Plus, of course,
a tonne packed away
for when there's no sun.
A day we all know
awaits.

For this concept to go
from state to state,
we need to love.
Not hate,
and to realise we all share
a mandatory fate.

If someone chooses to argue and gloat
while I sit and contemplate,
I'll honour their choice.
If they honour mine.
Then things can be just fine.

If we all just agree
that there's enough
for you,
and enough for me.

Then together
we'll speak
to let people
know, as for the
little folks,
they'll have
more of the same.

Listen here,
we can give up this
stupid game.
Drop the shame.
Stop thinking
different is wrong,
that we all have to be
alike or it can never
be right.

You just be you.
I'll just be me.
It will be diverse
and unity.

Passion in a Pill

What do I want?
What do I need?

passion in a pill,
love on line
youth in a bottle

money
success
speed

What do I want?
What I need.

instant gratification
everything now

no waiting
no thinking
no learning

deep fried
with onion rings

virtual lives
hologram companions
dehydrated
wet dreams

What I want.
What I need.

warm place to sleep
and well fed
there's no gunfire
to interrupt my dreams

someone to snuggle up close with
a friend to share a toast
all the tender joys in my life
that hold me, hold close.

How to Teach a Woman a Lesson

Sitting in a small office, she looked through books, volumes of faces.
Following your directions, trying to find clues... marks or a pox,
anything you said, so she could place her hand, really, just a mere finger
on a page. All this to bring a face from her nightmares to you.

Will this picture show his razor sharp eyes that cut her flesh?
Or, his sneer that left her teeth on the sidewalk?
Will this photo show how he took a drag off a cigarette before using
it to burn her?

The anger, the words, you and your blue knights show.
She cried, she puked, she bathed. All this has upset you so.

You sit and complain, you can locate his litter, but not him.
You strip her, poke her, and have her pose with her bruises.
Your demeanour is too, much, like his.
A call to her parents is your only solution.

Tarnished and torn, ripped from her, the soul is disengaged.
The answer to this, you say, is a hospital room.
A few pills will replenish her being.

You brought her in, but you could not make her stay.
The medical team, the psychiatrists, too,
They sat across from each other, and the words just flew.
She had enough of the theories, beliefs, unbalanced ideologies.
She exercised a right we all have. She got up and left.

She got on a plane and flew far away. No matter how far she travelled,
She never could leave.

So she sat down and faced it.
Alone in a field of sheep,
Which is the only protection anyone should ever need.

Her thoughts tell her this is backwards. We have it all wrong.
Two crimes occurred that night to one victim,
who was twice assaulted, once by a villian, and then by the law.

This is what she learned and she taught it to the lambs.
Your beatings have made her stronger.
Trying to silence her has made her voice louder.
Holding her down has quickened her step.
All this is an essential part of her now.

Half Breed

Always a half,
never a whole
Always a part,
never an entire
…thing.
Cuisine,
…values.

Questioning,
worth,
cherished,
place,
ethnicity,
culture,
…love.

Children born to bring a
family closer
separate them even more.

What language do they speak?
Neither.
What name do they carry?
Neither.
Who do they look like?
Neither.

Where does a half breed belong?
Nowhere.

You'd think this child has two cultures,
but, they believe they have none.

With patience they learn
they are actually treasured by both sides.
Learning to stir
spices from
half of this
to half of that
to
create
an
entire
whole
unique
…being.

When We Had Peace

When we had peace,
the symbols of two
great religions
both made of
stone
stood side by side
and neither group
questioned the other's
location
or
existence.

When we had peace,
we ate the same meals
shared the same villages
walked the same streets
together,
in stride.

When we had peace,
we both agreed
on certain values
and that on some occasions
we each had to step aside.

When we had peace,
we spoke at the well together,
shared schools,
and agreed to follow basic rules.

When we had peace,
we both wanted it
and we never questioned
that we could exist
in any other way.

Jethro the Arab

Jethro the Arab,
a tall man
with a bushy
moustache
and a
Stetson hat.

He and his father both born
in the city where
a star appeared
above a manger.

He was born Jamal.
They changed his name
when he came over here.

Jethro's son
was delivered
next door, to the
Rodeo Hall of Fame.

Jethro drives
a Bronco,
worry beads
hang from
the rear-view mirror.

Cowboy boots to work,
sandals at this house,
his favourite meal is
spiced hummus
with jalapenos.

"Jethro, man
Where are you from?"

"Palestine."
And he is.

The Olive Seed

The Olive Seed,
both potent and durable
strengthens through its
smouldering heat
crushed seed,
heats the taboon
Taita Nour's black office
four walls lined with benches
women sit and chat
loaves of bread dough
carried in on their heads
now, resting on the floor
gossiping, cheering, and trading
they cook as they talk freely
mornings are made for women
above the entrance are my Father's initials
he built this space for his Mother
now his daughters cook
there with her
dough coated in zait and zaatar
onions
cooked on
rocks
covering a heated resin
an ancient cooking tool
Taita tosses the dough
she says to be free you must be fed

to feed an Arab you need only
a rock,
dough,
and of course, an
olive seed
she knows this to be true,
she's tested it thoroughly
Turks,
Englishmen,
now Jews
all who have come and said this land is theirs
but here in this place
she knows
this spot
is hers.

With an Eagle's Strength

Arabic has never been the language of my dreams.
My skin and hair drained of their olive skin origin,
taking my first steps into my Father's homeland,
I carry with me only his name,
and a passport embossed in pride of the soaring eagle.

My journey begins at a bridge,
I'm separated,
my eagle caged.
Alone, with an enemy I have never met and
experiencing for the first time
someone else's hand on my naked body.
She holds a gun and
our eyes lock.
Two strangers exchanging hatred.
I yearn to spit my objections into her face and
she senses this.

Sneering,
She knocks my knees apart with the butt of her rifle.
I think of my Taita,
a living photograph who awaits me
behind the guarded door.
I keep silent
endure.

Awakened by a single loud knock.
Two military trucks
outside our door
soldiers enter and they are
yelling in a language that
I alone cannot understand.

Chaos
Guns

Moussa, my age
dragged across the floor
his Mother runs to him
kisses him
begs
take me.
He's just a boy.
A black-laced boot
ends her cries.
Silencing the room
eagle is knocked out of the sky,
tossed aside
and ground into the floor.

A fortnight passes and
My journey's end is near.
Moussa
beaten, swollen, bruised
collapses in the street.
He says the talons of my nation
have shred his hopes.

I take his hand,
together we travel back over the bridge
leaving my Father's land.

A tethered bird perched upon my soul
part of me is ashamed
remaining still, and claim it as my own
knowing that now,
it, too, carries my Father's name.

Accidental Genocide

Israeli,
We think it means
chosen people.
But, it really means
Warrior of God.

Are we not all warriors of God?
Are we not all then Israelis?
The Armenians, Christians,
Moslems and Jews.
Aren't they one and the same?
By the simple definition of the
title?

Palestinian Flag,
believed to be a terrorist symbol.
Not so. Those who believe this
do not know that its colours are well chosen.
Green for the valleys.
Black for the wars.
Red for the unnecessary death,
and white for peace.
That must come.

Silent,
naked,
side by side.
No one can tell
the enemies apart.
The Olive skin,
black hair,
or their pride.

Both fight,
for land,
their God.
Each saying they fight for the universal light.

The struggle is over
and terror has begun.
The abused child,
is now the violent parent.
Striking,
venomously, planned
and at random.
Leaving the other
weak,
wounded,
cries unheard.

Buildings fall.
Children die.
terror reigns,
in all domains.

Who will be left?
After the struggle,
to crawl out from
under the rubble?

A choking hold
is killing
an entire culture.
The media
is exploiting
the demise of an entire race.

No longer are there weddings,
backgammon games are gone.
Olive trees bulldozed under.
A search for food,
for heat,
a daily struggle
to find one meal.
to feed,
to nourish
enough
to leave.

Fleeing to other lands,
children born into foreign hands.
Languages lost,
homeland forgotten,
fewer and fewer,
wish to stay.
The cause is now to just
get away.

The damage that is being done;
The deaths, the innocents dying,
the terror and the fear.
In the end, whose God
will have won?

Are we prepared?
For when the dust is settled,
the last bullet fired,
and the buildings crumbled.
When we go to tally up
the Palestinians
to find
that no one
remains.

The...
...laSt
...peArls
...oF
...wIsdOm

Dear Nora

Dear Nora,

In my mind birth and death are reciprocal actions. Before birth our mothers knew us. Together, we co-existed and we sensed each other. We communicated together with touch and emotions. We physically grew together. All this happens before a baby can even breathe on their own. They know their mother, her voice, her scent and her emotions. Then we live — at first our lives are our parents' memories, and then our own.

Finally, in death, we still emotionally exist in the minds of all the lives we've touched and cared for. Our energy is there, the consequences of our actions cannot be reversed. The love we have sowed is still blooming. Even though we are not still here physically on earth we still co-exist with these beings with whom we have interwoven our journeys. A bond with a woman and a child she has birthed is immeasurable through time and the love is infinite. This means you and I have always known each other. And we always will.

I Love You the Yellowest

Dear Mom,
I love you the yellowest.
You are the sun shining on our family that all
evolves around.
I admire your strength and endurance in the
chaos of our childhood.
What I admire most is the joy we so obviously
brought to you and how you radiated it back to
Us.
As the sun fades and sets, you too are
leaving.
You ensure for your children cherished
colours and inner tranquillity as it happens.
I will never again experience a sunset as
precious as you are to me.

We are ready now for night to fall,

Before you go, I want you to know that
I will always love you the yellowest.

Skinny Dippin' with My Holy Man

Hot water generated from a **CAVE.**
Five volcanic pools, heated by the warmth of friendship.

Cap_tur_ing
(cedar leaves-redwood trunks-crisp air-a limestone carving)
> *Slide*
> *In…*

> Sit on a natural bench of rocks
> Water right   smiles
> below   all
> the chin   around.

Skinny dipping with my holy man.

A	*A*
FULL	*or new*
Moon	*Moon*

It doesn't matter,
It's about how two friends
Cherish the other.
Sharing an unmentioned modesty of love.

Touching
looking,
not even a thought.
Just love and attention
talking or not.

Silence,
too, is precious.
as one speaks the other's thoughts,
Words comfort
looks and exchanges
both
relax
and
refresh...

.

.

.

... as each finds the other
                        ...divine...

The Moment Before Our First Kiss

The moment before
our first kiss
before our lips
ever touched.

Millenniums of
passion
brought us
together.

Life went on
as it always has
as it always will.

Vows were said
decisions made
babies raised.

Chores were done,
grace was spoken and
travels made.

Actions powered by fate
from year one to
now
every instant
led,
guided,
and directed;
this moment
to me.

Being
here
with you.

Boodles

For that's what I call you when I think of you.
For a shot of the laughter, the wit and the joy.
Boodles.
It's indeed true that having you around makes everything better.

I want to open the bottle.
Rejoice in the sweet pink of conversation and cooking.
Boodles.
Your sudden smile unseals an aura of relaxing intoxication.

Anticipating tanginess of delight touching the lips.
My cravings overwhelm my fears.
Boodles.
A future moment awaits in a night cap to be savoured.

Perhaps, one day we will have that drink.
A simple sip to squelch a longing.
Boodles.
A refreshing moment for exhilarating thirst.

Poetry and Love

What is the link between poetry and love? I lay awake at
night and look out into the stars and wonder if the reason
they are so far from the earth is because they have never felt
love.

I have travelled love's journey. The path I chose is a
rocky one. A rocky path lincurs no footprints. No tracks, no
marks to let anyone know this path was even travelled.
Only the one who has walked it knows the journey took place.

Rocky climbs are almost always uphill. At the top is a view
that few have ever seen. Even those who venture out in
helicopters cannot experience it as the rock climber has.

For them the journey to that spot was a struggle. Yet, only for the
climber, not the rock; two elements of nature, one powered by
a motivation that cannot be named.

The other silent, at rest,
knowing for centuries all life is carved from the wonders of
the earth. Once that is known, the only option left is to be still.
Let other life forms come to you, teach and guide them by
letting your warmth soak through their fingertips. Allow step
holds placed by time to lift them up to the next level.
This is love.

The journey's tale, this is poetry.

Muse

When life is too hard, I go to the ocean. Alone, at the
edge of biological surge, my view is an endless sky. I place
my bare feet into the water. The waves caress my toes, and
my feet sink into the sand as I let this natural cadence
encompass me. The tides refresh and cleanse and that is all
that matters. Only recreating this moment between me and the
sea has ever had this effect. This ended when I saw the Muse
dance. This being cannot be summoned, yet knows when to
appear. Physically, she was dancing with another, but a gleam,
a glow in her eye, helped me discover she was dancing with
me. Gently, when the music was done, and the food put away,
Placed her hand on my pulse and for the first time I felt
my own rhythm. Awakened by the caress of every soul
lapping from the well of creativity; water that exists in us all.
In an instant of touch, an orgasm of the mind, transformed by
a sip of red wine; liquor of life. One taste of this nectar
intoxicates an entire being. For many their potential slips
away, unrecognised, untouched; the waste of a miracle. When
this tragedy is near, the muse must emerge.

Who would not wish for this partner to stay, as she
loves like no other. Creation produced all; some speculate that
the most miraculous is the muse. Remembering the vision of
witnessing her perform a simple task, the sole reason for her

existence; inspiration. Drawn in by candlelight, warm tea, quiet moments, it is believed that she seeks visionaries with powerful passions. Always, she moves of her own free will. Yes, once she arrives, drawing her in is possible. However, only she can decide to stay.

Poets Are Faggots

Poets.
Are faggots.
They are weak and powerless.
Living in a dream world,
out of touch with reality.

Harm.
No one,
but have no use.
Who'd ever want their child to be
a creature like this?

People.
Who'd go into a battle
armed only with words.
A person who leads rebellions
from a podium.
One human who can make another cry,
by simply reciting verse.

Ask.
Who will listen to these people?
Who will notice a single soliloquy
or respond to their pleas?

Demand.
Who are they?
Where do they come from?
Where shall we keep them?
Do we need them?

Actualize.
If they were gone.
there'd be no secrets shared
or love confided.
Who'd embrace the winds
or kiss the stars good-night?

Create.
An absence of matter. A void,
an emotional awakening.
Forcing us to consider;
Can we live without them?

Remind.
All that is owed to these
Gentle wandering souls.
The pleasures they have pointed out
and pains they have averted.

Discover.
A passion ignited by a small kiss.
The opera in the sunrise.
The raised maze grown in a cedar tree
and feel the grass between the toes.

Notice.
The reflection of the moon on a still lake.
Aroma of a home-cooked meal.
A lover's touch.
A widow's grief.
Footsteps on a playground.

Gift.
Of words.
These and more,
Found in the reservoir of every poet's heart.
Energy to be released by pen and ink.

Confessions

I must confess as I sit with a poet's sword in hand, that I do not write poetry. Not one word is mine. I merely reside in one spot, my flesh a receptor of all swirling about, absorbing messages and feelings; in tune to a power stronger than all of us, yet, able to be pushed away by a single moment of doubt.

My heart feels what every heart feels. My eyes see what all eyes see and my body reacts to your pain.

Faith is founded in me at a cellular level. My mind stores the knowledge of the ancients and my heart holds the whispered promises of hope.

My hand cups the wisdom of truth that we all share: the power to forgive.

I must confess, among this perfection is a flaw. My mouth; afraid to speak and share this awareness. Closed in a timid silence, lips locked by the fear of how others will react to this knowledge.

I sit silent... writing what I am afraid to speak.

Fear of Poetry

What we fear the most,
may be what ultimately frees us.

My one desire is to kiss my grandmother's hand
before death claims her.

Once this is done,
I'll forever know,
wherever my journey takes me,
I travel under her blessings.

That is important to me'
as I journey I take a part of her
with me, and she will take
a part of me with her.

Life and poetry are one
and the same.
A series of poems
is a sequence of moments,
the breath of life
flows off the page.

Recapture.
Share,
Give the moment to others
as you
cover them from harm
with a piece of your soul.

Valour is shown
as one shares the spoken word.

Yet, as I declare myself a poet,
it is the recipient of my message
who deems me worthy of the title.

Dedications

There are several people who inspired me or to whom I wish to dedicate the poems within this book:

'Wood Stove' is dedicated to my Father, Fuad Saleh.

'Stuck' was inspired by Ms. Katherine Maser, fourth grade teacher extraordinaire.

'Manure' is dedicated with affection to all who have ever held the postal address Amery, WI 54001.

'To the Women of the Central Point Twins Creek Outside Class' is dedicated to the beautiful community of Central Point, OR.

'Lessons from My Singing Teacher' is dedicated to Frazer Scott. A gifted teacher, singer, brideperson, friend, and colleague.

'Lennon's Paradise' is dedicated to Dustin Shulte and Daniel Smelling who were two good men and friends who died untimely deaths.

'The Olive Seed' was inspired by my Grandmother, Nur Saleh, who in turn inspired generations with a century of love and good cooking.

"Dear Nora' is dedicated to Carol and Nora McKinley.

'I Love You the Yellowest' is dedicated to my Mother, Helen Saleh.

'Skinny Dippin' with My Holy Man' is dedicated to Dan Orleck, who has always been generous with his friendship and advice.

'Boodles' is dedicated to everyone who overcame heartbreak and dared to hope to connect with someone again.

About the Author

Lisa Nora Saleh is a Palestinian-American poet who was born in Boston, Massachusetts on the very first Earth Day and raised in the Mid-West. Educated at Clark University (BA), Northland College (BSc), Goddard College (MA), and Southern Oregon University (MSC), she currently resides in the Pacific Northwest after almost twenty years in the United Kingdom. She first writes her poetry by playing her thoughts on her flute, and she has been writing this way each summer at Lithia Park in Southern Oregon for more than two decades. Saleh has been a guest editor for *Sable Literature Magazine*; an international playwright, including for several seasons at the International Dublin LGBT Theatre Festival; as well as a travelling storyteller; and a teacher.

CPSIA information can be obtained
at www.ICGtesting.com
Printed in the USA
BVHW041039181221
624353BV00002B/256